Real Rhyming Poems

Real Rhyming Poems

by

J. M. Allen

© 2022 J. M. Allen. All rights reserved.
This material may not be reproduced in any form, published,
reprinted, recorded, performed, broadcast,
rewritten or redistributed without
the explicit permission of J. M. Allen.
All such actions are strictly prohibited by law.

Cover design by Shay Culligan
Cover image by Stephen Cassara

ISBN: 978-1-63980-128-2

Kelsay Books
502 South 1040 East, A-119
American Fork, Utah 84003
Kelsaybooks.com

For everyone who enjoys rhyming poetry

Acknowledgments

These poems appeared in the following publications.

Adelaide Literary Magazine: "Genes," "Why I Bought A Gun," and "Drivers Test"

The Asses of Parnassus: "Cold"

Bluing the Blade: "Rabbit," "Cards"

Grand Little Things: "Phone and TV," "Dumb Drivers"

Instant Noodles: "Statue"

Lighten Up Online: "Open Question"

The Parliament Lit Journal: "The Lawn Keeper"

Poetry Potion: "Straight A's"

Post Bulletin (newspaper) and AP: "Ten Hours of Sleep"

Rhyme & Rhythm (anthology): "The Drive Home"

Rue Scribe: "An E-mail Never Sent," "Dragon"

Tiny Seed Literary Journal: "Bergamot"

Wingless Dreamer: "Playground," "The Waves," and "Empty Grave"

Contents

Open Question	11
Cold	12
Statue	13
Coins	14
Dandelions	15
Rabbit	16
Cards	17
The Lawn Keeper	18
Playground	19
The Drive Home	20
Youth Sports Referee	21
Straight A's	22
Acknowledgment	23
Bergamot	24
The Narrow Paths	25
The Waves	26
Eruption	27
Phone and TV	28
An E-mail Never Sent	29
Genes	30
Why I Bought a Gun	31
Drivers Test	32
One Mistake	33
Maintenance	34
Dumb Drivers	35
Living at the Hospital	36
Empty Grave	37
The Snowperson	38
Ten Hours of Sleep	39
Dragon	40

Open Question

The first snow of winter—isn't it great?
I left extra early, so I wouldn't be late.
The best season is…I can't decide which.
I debate as my car is pulled from a ditch.

Cold

Ah, life in Minnesota,
in the summer it's such a breeze.
But if you don't wear a hat in winter,
your ears will likely freeze.

Statue

The statue in the garden,
peaceful and silent.
The fountain nearby,
splashing and violent.

The statue is in the center,
cast in concrete.
Surrounded by flowers,
brilliant and sweet.

The statue stares blankly,
like a bold thief.
It doesn't have to converse,
what a relief.

Coins

I miss acquiring coins
Collecting each state quarter
Now my transactions are on-line
Where no checkout line is shorter

No longer kept in my pocket
Where they gave a walking jingle
Few coins on the ground to pick up
Their discovery would give a tingle

But coins aren't coming back
With less every year hence
Gathered by fewer people
Which only makes cents

Dandelions

It's the sharp contrast of color,
yellow against green.
That makes their presence so glaring,
in my front yard scene.

Lawn mowing removes the heads,
but they soon grow back.
My neighbors war against them,
yet weed chemicals I lack.

Their seeds start sprouting,
after rain showers.
So if you don't want to see them,
come pick the flowers.

Rabbit

I see him at my garden
A cottontail rabbit
Munching my green beans again
His frequent summer habit

His cuteness may fool you
Yet my dismay is non-stopping
And I assume he knows that
From the taunts in his hopping

I sneaked closer to scare him
That sly long-eared bunny
But he escaped me quite easily
Which he probably finds funny

Cards

Play the hands that you were dealt,
was the main lesson given to me.
Keep them close to your chest,
so that others cannot see.
Keep an ace in the hole,
for as long as you can.
Getting a straight flush,
can't be your only plan.
I said thanks for the tips,
and I'll keep up my guards.
But I wondered when someone
would teach me how to play cards?

The Lawn Keeper

Early on Sunday mornings,
my neighbor is out mowing his lawn.
I'm still in bed trying to sleep,
because it is not long past dawn.

He patrols his whole lawn daily,
the grass is a thick dark green.
Automatic sprinklers run daily,
and there is not a weed to be seen.

Chemicals are often sprayed on it,
and I think ants get it the worst.
No insects at all are tolerated,
even though they lived there first.

The weed trimmer is very loud,
and the cordless blower too.
Much energy spent fighting nature,
all for one home owner's view.

Playground

I walked to the playground
Many fun things there to do
Climb on the monkey bars
And go on the swings too

Time was passing by me fast
Until I got the cruel insult
The mom asked me to leave
Saying it's not meant for an adult

The Drive Home

The game just ended, and I did a few things bad.
Now for the drive home, and hearing from my dad.
While he drives the car, he goes over every misstep.
And do I agree with an analysis? I just say "Yep".

On each mistake, I'm told what I should have done.
And it doesn't matter whether our team lost or won!
He hopes he can teach me, and maybe he might?
Just agreeing with him is better than putting up a fight.

It matters so much more to him than it does to me.
He records my game stats for something for him to see.
He has expectations for where my game skills are headed.
But if only dad knew: how much the drive home is dreaded.

Youth Sports Referee

I've been a youth sports referee
But the parents like to yell at me
I can't see everything, and I can make mistakes
These games are only held for the kids' sakes

If I get screamed at again, I'll end my officiating journey
And there won't be enough refs to hold the spring tourney
Here goes another dad lecturing me on a decision
He should instead imagine himself in my position

Straight A's

I've gotten straight A's so far, I'm a sophomore in high school.
But they haven't helped me yet, in fact made me un-cool.
I want to compete for grades, but no one else really cares.
And so when I hand in extra credit, all I get is stares.

I wish it was like sports, where everyone tries to beat others.
People would congratulate the best grade, if I had my druthers.
They could all give high-fives, on a test where I dominate.
But they don't praise the grade winner, they'd rather just hate.

Everyone would want to be like me, I'd be the hero.
But instead it's the opposite, they see me as a zero.
I have to face the facts, and come back from outer space:
Tests just don't compare to sports—in getting first place.

Acknowledgment

If you smile and say hi, it just might brighten my day.
Or nod to me when passing, nothing you need to say.
When I'm driving my route, a wave to me would be niceness.
And you may make me smile, a feeling that is priceless.

Bergamot

Every mid-summer July blooms the wild bergamot.
And in southeast Minnesota, it often is found a lot.
The round flowers are lavender-ish pink.
Come out to the prairie and see what you think.

It has a minty smell, and the bees like to visit them.
They are about a yard long, to the end of their stem.
They are often found in groups or bunches.
Come out to the prairie and bring your lunches.

The coneflowers also bloom about the same time.
Show me your favorites, and I'll show you mine.
Glad it's a native plant, not an invasive pest.
Come out to the prairie and see it in its best!

The Narrow Paths

I like to hike on the narrow paths
With trees and plants close to me
Not the wide and clear trails
Where nature is further to see

I trek in the morning to avoid others
Their noise and trash I abhor
Nature can help to evade people
But every year there is more!

Wonderful is the fresh air
It smells best by the pine
The scent is more intoxicating
Than any bottle of wine

The Waves

I stand on the beach
And stare at my foes
The white caps are crashing
Down by my toes

I walk into the water
Waves try to push me around
The long battle begins
With their roaring sound

I taste their sprays
As I wade in deeper
Stepping on broken shells
Placed by the great sweeper

I fight their forces
My war instinct is tapped
And I won't give up
Until my strength is sapped

Eruption

My boss micro-manages
And delivers slights too
That causes me anger
But I have not yet blew

I swallow the magma
Instead of letting it vent
If the lava flowed freely
Hatred would be spent

So I hold back an eruption
Feeling quite bloated
While I patiently wait
Until he gets promoted

Phone and TV

When I watch TV, my phone is always in my hand.
And every time there's a dull moment, I do a quick scan.
I think it's low probability, on the show something key that I miss.
But sometimes later I find out—it often was the main plot twist.

I don't seem to learn, that next time I focus on the show.
But TV can't keep my attention, it's just way too slow.
I need my phone in my hand, scan the news to get the facts.
Without it I could be missing something, it's hard to just relax.

I can't watch a whole movie, without glancing at my phone.
If I don't check it occasionally, I feel so very alone.
I cycle through the same apps, something new usually on some.
Because if you have a phone, you never have to suffer boredom.

An E-mail Never Sent

I wrote an e-mail; it was how I reacted.
I was about to hit Send, but a text got me distracted.
The content came to me fast, as my anger slowly rose.
I just kept on typing, with the sharp words that I chose.

I detailed my complaint, didn't leave anything out.
It got very detailed; put in everything I could think about.
I wanted it to be clear, I wanted it to be concise.
But one thing I didn't try, that was to be nice.

I would have sent it, if it wasn't for my phone.
But I like to get notifications, especially if I'm alone.
And so after the delay, my draft e-mail I re-read.
And then it struck me—I should just call him instead!

Genes

I am stuck this way, there's no way to change me it seems.
Because this physical characteristic, it is due to my genes.
I crave to fit in! But I'm obviously different as you see.
My parents didn't consider what burdens that it would have on me.

From before I was born, I was to inherit my trait.
There's nothing I can do—I am stuck with my fate.
There is no path to normal, it really isn't fair.
And I hate it when people sometimes gawk and stare.

Almost all people are so fortunate and don't even know.
The DNA is on the inside, but on the outside it may show.
If I had just one wish, I sure know what I'd say.
Just to be ordinary! If only just for one day.

Why I Bought a Gun

Guns are made to hurt people,
that is clear for everyone to see.
So I bought myself a firearm,
to deter someone from shooting me.
Yes I believe I'm going to go to Heaven,
which is a Paradise that is quite fair.
But I'd rather kill someone who was trying
the same to me—and thus to not go there.

Drivers Test

Put away your phone, and we will go outside.
Hop in my car, and I'll take us for a ride.
Driving starts out nice with few vehicles around.
Turn on some music and listen to the sound.

But as we head downtown, traffic starts to get thick.
And the smell of exhaust, it makes me feel slightly sick.
The greenish view has slowly changed to concrete.
After a short while, I wish I could get out of my seat.

The many red lights, they all last way too long.
And the fun of steering, it has long since been gone.
My car now tests my sanity, where it used to be the best.
Should I get rid of my prime possession? The real drivers test.

One Mistake

Making just one mistake,
might forever impact your life.
It can cost you your job,
and cause other types of strife.

You would never repeat it again,
yet no way to wipe the slate clean.
Why can't you get a second chance?
Sometimes experience can be mean.

Probably no way to free yourself,
from a digitally tagged snare.
Since life can be so regretful,
do what you can to make it fair.

Maintenance

I'd like to throw my toothbrush away
But dental pain may have the last say
And I don't feel like checking any filter
Even if an appliance might get off kilter
I'd like to quit the oil changes for my car
Although after a while it won't go very far
I wish I could start to let my grass grow long
My neighbors soon reveal something's wrong
And I could just ignore requests from my friends
But when I need some help - nobody to aid my ends

I just want to sit on the couch with my phone and chill
Yet there are tasks that could use attention still
Seems something always needs to be done
Maintenance itself is never won

Dumb Drivers

My back hurts again, not sure what I should do.
The hours spent on the road really sneak up on you.
If it wasn't for the dumb drivers, I would arrive much faster.
The other motorists are foolish or stupid, it really doesn't matter.

And these dummies are everywhere,
and are all seeming to journey far.
Although I'll need their help—
as I've locked my phone and keys in my car.

Living at the Hospital

I'm mostly living at the hospital,
sure wish I could be done.
I keep needing to give my birth date,
my life should be more fun.

Another medical procedure,
another medical test.
Another doctor visit,
each just like the rest.

The waiting rooms grow old,
along with myself.
I sometimes read the labels
of the items on the shelf.

The problem reason is genetic,
that my health is so brittle.
Meaning that it came from my parents,
who I can't cease to blame a little.

Empty Grave

Sometimes when I go walking
I stroll through the cemetery
Which seems just like a big park
With no need to be wary

I saw a grave lay open
But the tombstone was old
There were splinters of wood
And it smelled bad like mold

Nearby vases were smashed
All the debris made me tense
A sudden fear of the graveyard
Good thing it has a fence

The Snowperson

During the first snow of winter
I went for a walk after work
Already a snowperson was built
Its face held a vexing smirk

A tall green pointy hat
Made it resembling a witch
I felt a sudden cold wind
Up from the nearby ditch

It seemed the head turned
And the stick arms reached
As if trying to get me
My confidence breached

I caught it glaring at me
Giving me a frown
And I hope I don't regret
Having knocked it down

Ten Hours of Sleep

I want ten hours of sleep, but don't know when I will.
Just be able to stay in bed, laying perfectly still.
When you have young kids, you keep getting woke up.
Someone keeps crying, or another wants a sippy cup.

I've gotten so tired, of the morning alarm chime.
Should I call in sick? I've thought that many a time.
I feel so comfortable, wrapped in my cozy bed.
But I make myself get up, my eyes still showing red.

Even on weekends, there's too much going on.
My to-do list is long, need to wake up with the sun.
So I force myself to do stuff, aware of the pleasure delay.
In the future I will sleep in—can't wait until that fine day.

Dragon

I'll need to persevere—not give up again.
I'm going to start now—stop debating when.

I've decided anew to accept the fight.
I'll summon all my internal might.

I've got my sword, and I've got my shield.
I'll ride steed across the open field.

The smoke is still visible, a distance away.
Up in a mountain, too high some say.

To calm my nerves, a drink from my flagon.
And I promise this time, to slay my dragon.

About the Author

J. M. Allen is an electrical engineer and parent, who enjoys writing rhyming poems.

He is a graduate of the University of Michigan, and has been a long-time resident of Rochester, Minnesota.

Made in the USA
Monee, IL
21 October 2025